Collins

easy learning

Problem solving and reasoning

Ages 5–7

ICE CREAM

Rachel Axten-Higgs

How to use this book

- Find a quiet, comfortable place to work, away from other distractions.

- Make sure your child has some paper to write their ideas and working on.

- This book takes a thematic approach to problem solving and reasoning. Tackle one theme at a time.

- Within each theme there are lots of problem-solving and reasoning activities for your child to complete. Your child will have to select and apply the appropriate number, measurement and / or geometry skills to solve each problem.

- Help with reading the instructions where necessary and ensure that your child understands what to do.

- If your child is struggling with a particular activity, discuss with them what they know, what they need to find out and how they might go about it.

- Help and encourage your child to check their own answers as they complete each activity.

- Discuss with your child what they have learnt.

- Let your child return to their favourite pages once they have been completed, to talk about the activities.

- Reward your child with plenty of praise and encouragement.

Special features

- Yellow boxes: introduce each theme.

- Orange boxes: contain different problem-solving and reasoning activities based on the theme.

- Orange shaded boxes: offer advice to parents on how to support their child's learning.

ACKNOWLEDGEMENTS

Published by Collins
An imprint of HarperCollins*Publishers*
1 London Bridge Street
London SE1 9GF

© HarperCollins*Publishers* Limited 2018

ISBN 9780008275358

10 9 8 7 6 5

British Library Cataloguing in Publication Data

A Catalogue record for this publication is available from the British Library

Author: Rachel Axten-Higgs
Commissioning editor: Michelle l'Anson
Editor and project manager: Rebecca Skinner
Cover design: Sarah Duxbury
Interior concept design: Ian Wrigley
Page layouts: Q2A Media Services PVT Ltd.
Production: Lyndsey Rogers
Printed in Great Britain by Martins the Printers

MIX
Paper from responsible source
FSC www.fsc.org
FSC™ C007454

This book is produced from independently certified FSC™ paper to ensure responsible forest management.

For more information visit:
www.harpercollins.co.uk/green

Contents

Travelling by bus

Today you are travelling on a bus.
The bus makes lots of different stops to pick up and drop off people.

1 The bus has 2 floors.
Each floor holds 10 people.

How many people can fit on the bus in total? ☐ people

2 You are on the bus.
There are two other people on the bus.
At the first bus stop, 4 people get **on**.

How many people are now on the bus? $1 + 2 + 4 =$ 7 people

3 There are 14 people on the bus.
At the next bus stop, 6 people get **off**.

How many people are on the bus now? $14 - 6 =$ ☐ people

You can help your child to represent the calculations by using concrete objects to represent the people, e.g. you could use their toys for the people and a piece of card for the bus. Your child can physically move the people on and off the bus to help them solve the problem.

4 There are this many people on the bus:

There are this many people waiting at the bus stop:

The people at the bus stop get **on** the bus.

Write a number sentence to show how many people are on the bus now and work out the answer.

_____

There are this many people on the bus:

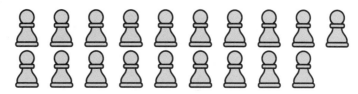

This many people get **off** the bus at the next stop:

Write a number sentence to show how many people are on the bus now and work out the answer.

_____

5 There are two buses.
One bus has 16 people on it.
The other bus has 12 people on it.

Use the number line to count on from 16 to find how many people are on the two buses in total.

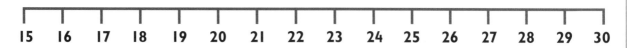

| | | | | | | | | | | | | | | | |
15 16 17 18 19 20 21 22 23 24 25 26 27 28 29 30

[   ] people

Going to a cafe

In a cafe, there are numbers all around you – the number of people at tables, the prices of food and drink and the number of slices that a cake is divided into.

1 You are sitting at a table with your family.

There are 4 of you at the table.
There are 12 other customers in the cafe.

How many customers are in the

cafe in total? ☐ customers

3 more customers come into the cafe.

How many customers are in the cafe now? ☐ customers

2 There are enough chairs in the cafe for 20 customers.
On Monday, 9 chairs have customers sitting on them.

How many more customers can sit in the cafe? ☐ customers

On Tuesday, all the chairs are full.
4 customers get up and leave.

How many customers are now sitting on chairs? ☐ customers

To help your child understand the calculations they need to perform, use counters to represent people and paper squares for the chairs. Your child can then physically move the people on and off the chairs. They can then put the people in lines to count them before moving on to a written calculation.

3 The cakes are in 2 fridges.
There are 8 cakes in each fridge.

How many cakes are there in total?

☐ cakes

One large cake is cut into 12 slices.
A lady buys 5 slices of the cake.

How many slices of the cake are left?

☐ slices

A man buys 7 slices of chocolate cake and 6 slices of carrot cake.

How many slices of cake does he buy altogether?

☐ slices

Medium cakes are cut into 5 slices.
A lady buys 4 medium cakes.

How many slices of cake does she have altogether?

☐ slices

4 Doughnuts come in boxes of 5.
A man buys 3 boxes of doughnuts.

How many doughnuts does he have altogether?

☐ doughnuts

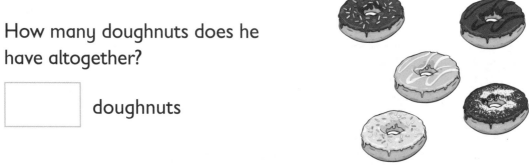

5 The cafe serves 2 slices of toast with every cooked breakfast.

On Monday, the cafe serves 10 cooked breakfasts.

How many slices of toast does it serve with cooked breakfasts in total? ⬜ slices of toast

One man wants to double the number of slices of toast with his cooked breakfast.

How many slices of toast will he get? ⬜ slices of toast

There are 3 mushrooms in each cooked breakfast.

On Tuesday, the cafe serves 5 cooked breakfasts.

How many mushrooms does it serve? ⬜ mushrooms

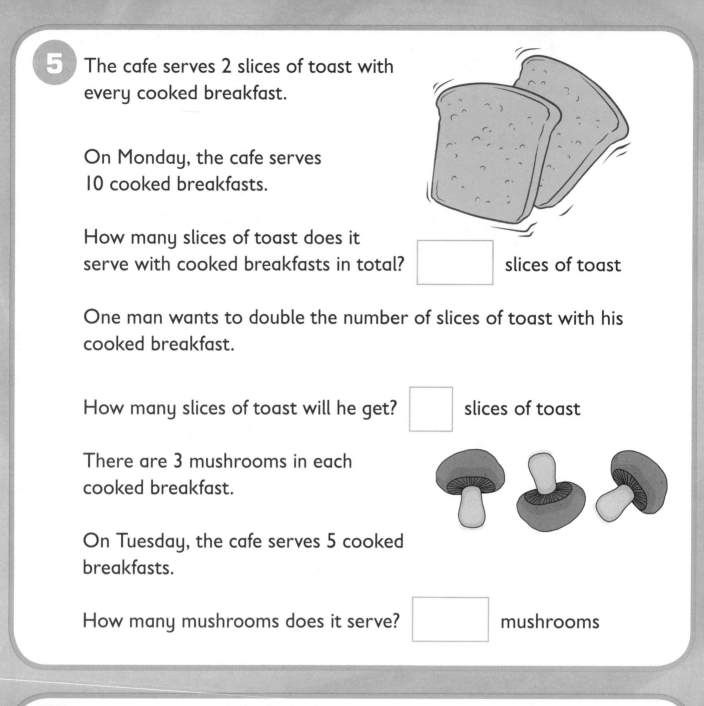

6 In one week, the cafe uses 18 boxes of eggs.
They want to order half this number as they will be closed for a few days next week.

How many boxes of eggs should they order? ⬜ boxes

7 You are at the cafe for a friend's birthday party.
There are 6 chairs at the table.
Each chair has 2 balloons tied to it.

How many balloons are there altogether?

[ ] balloons

There are 6 children and 5 adults at the party.
The cafe has a total of 20 chairs.
All the children and adults at the party sit on chairs.

How many chairs are left for other customers? [ ] chairs

8 Your friend's birthday cake is cut into
16 pieces.

All the children and adults at the party
have one slice of cake each.

How many slices of cake are left? [ ] slices

9 The cafe provides 6 cookies with sweets on.
There are 5 sweets on each cookie.

How many sweets are on all the cookies in total?

[ ] sweets

The cookies cost £2 each.

How much is spent on cookies for the party? £ [ ]

Going on a country walk

You are out for a walk in the countryside.
There are lots of things to see including flowers, insects and animals.

1 You see 10 cows in a field.
5 of the cows are black.
5 of the cows are brown.

Tick the fraction of the cows
that are black.

$\frac{1}{4}$ ☐ $\frac{1}{3}$ ☐ $\frac{1}{2}$ ☐ $\frac{3}{4}$ ☐

2 Your family has brought a pie to eat on the walk.
It has been cut into 4 equal pieces.
You eat one of the pieces.

How much of the pie have you eaten?

$\frac{1}{4}$ ☐ $\frac{1}{3}$ ☐ $\frac{1}{2}$ ☐ $\frac{3}{4}$ ☐

3 You pick a long piece of grass.
It is 12 cm long.
You tear it exactly in half.

How long is each piece of grass? ☐ cm

To help your child understand the concept of $\frac{1}{2}$, $\frac{1}{4}$, $\frac{1}{3}$ and $\frac{3}{4}$, it is important to give them objects to play with (e.g. counters, toys or stones). For example, they can count out the total and then divide into two equal groups to find out what half the quantity is. This is a good activity for outdoors as well.

4 You find a stick.
It is 60 cm long.
You want to break it in half to play with.

How long will each piece be? ☐ cm

5 You find 15 ladybirds.
5 of them have 8 spots.

What fraction of the ladybirds has 8 spots?

$\frac{1}{2}$ ☐ $\frac{1}{3}$ ☐ $\frac{1}{4}$ ☐ $\frac{3}{4}$ ☐ $\frac{2}{4}$ ☐

6 You find a small pond with 16 fish in it.

What fraction of the fish are orange?

$\frac{1}{2}$ ☐ $\frac{1}{4}$ ☐ $\frac{1}{3}$ ☐

$\frac{3}{4}$ ☐ $\frac{2}{4}$ ☐

7 You see 12 goats in a field.
6 of the goats are white.
Your mum says, "$\frac{2}{4}$ of the goats in the field are white."

Is she correct?   yes ☐   no ☐

Explain your answer.

_____

_____

Going on holiday

You are going on holiday today!
You need to be able to tell the time so that you don't miss your ferry.
You also need to be able to use coins so that you can buy things with your holiday money.

1 You have to wake up early to get to the ferry on time.
Your mum says you need to wake up at quarter past 6 in the morning.

Draw hands on the clock to show this time.

When you wake up, the clock shows this time:

Have you woken up early or late?

early ☐   late ☐

You and your family leave the house at 7 o'clock in the morning.
You have to travel by car to the ferry port.

It takes $3\frac{1}{2}$ hours.

Draw hands on the clock to show the time you arrive.

Talking about time with your child is really important. When you are out or preparing to go out, talk to them about the time and show them the hands on the clock. This will help them to become familiar with the concept of time intervals.

2 At 12 o'clock you board the ferry.
You have 25 minutes until it leaves.

Draw hands on the clock
to show what time the ferry will leave.

The ferry journey takes $2\frac{1}{2}$ hours.

What time will you arrive?
Use your answer above as the start time for the journey.

_____

3 On the ferry you read a sign that says there are 2 decks of cars.

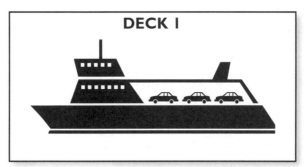

DECK 1

One deck holds 40 cars and the other deck holds 60 cars.

How many cars can the ferry hold? ☐ cars

The first deck has 7 empty spaces.
The second deck has 13 empty spaces.

How many empty spaces are there in total? ☐ empty spaces

How many cars are on board the ferry? ☐ cars

4 You arrive at your holiday home.
You go for a swim in the pool at quarter past 6 in the evening.
You swim for 40 minutes.

What time do you finish swimming? _____

You begin eating dinner at half past 7.
You finish the meal at 5 minutes past 8.

Did you spend longer eating or swimming?

eating ☐   swimming ☐

5 You have £10 holiday money to spend.
You buy a beautiful shell for £1.

How much money do you have left? £ ☐

You gave the shopkeeper two coins to make £1.
One of the coins was a 50p.

What was the other coin? Circle the correct option.

Draw another combination of coins you could have used to make £1.

Help your child to understand that different combinations of coins can make the same total. Play games using real coins so that they understand their values. For example, give them two 1p coins and ask them to find another coin that is equal to the total of these – a 2p coin.

6 You buy a postcard to send to your friend.
The postcard costs 25p.
You also buy a stamp for 65p.

How much do you spend altogether? [ ] p

You buy a crabbing line, bucket and bait.
The total cost is 4 pounds and 10 pence.
You give the shopkeeper £5.

How much change do you get back? [ ] p

You have £4 of your holiday money left.
You look at these items in the toy shop:

| 80p | 50p | £2 | 95p | £3 |

If you bought the teddy, could you also buy the sweet jar?

yes [ ]   no [ ]

Explain your answer.

_____

If you bought the sweet jar, could you also buy the toy plane?

yes [ ]   no [ ]

Explain your answer.

_____

Visiting the zoo

Today you are visiting the zoo.
Your teacher has given you a map of the zoo.
She has asked you to look out for different shapes around the zoo.

1 You are standing at **A** with your back to the bear cage.
Make a quarter turn anticlockwise.
Walk in a straight line and then make another quarter turn anticlockwise.

Which animal is in front of you?

_____

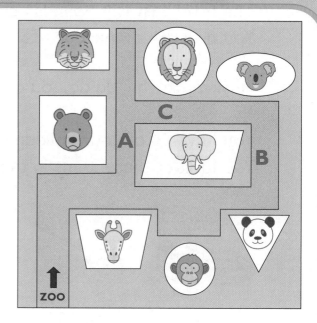

You are standing at **B** facing the elephants.
Make a quarter turn clockwise and walk in a straight line.

Which animal is in front of you? _____

You are standing at **C** facing the lion cage.

Write the turns and forward movements you would have to make if you wanted to face the panda.

_____

_____

2 Look at the map and answer the following questions.

Which animals are in enclosures that are circles?

_____

How many types of animal are in enclosures that have four sides?

What shape is the enclosure that the giraffes are in?

_____

Does the koala bear enclosure have any lines of symmetry?

yes ☐   no ☐

Explain how you know?

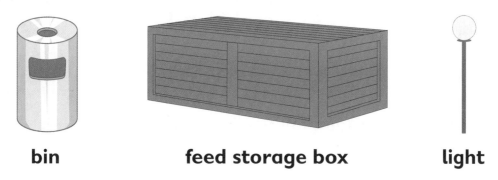

_____

_____

Draw the line of symmetry on the panda enclosure.

3 Your teacher points out some of the objects around the zoo:

bin   **feed storage box**   **light**

Which object is a sphere? _____

Write the shape of the object that has 6 faces, 8 vertices and 12 edges.

_____

What shape is the bin and how many edges does it have?

_____

4 The zoo has a play area with a large climbing frame.
The climbing frame has two large towers.
Each tower is a cuboid with a square-based pyramid on top.

What 2-D shapes make up the faces of the:

square-based pyramid? _____

cuboid? _____

The two towers are joined by a shape that has six rectangles and two hexagons as its faces.

What is the name of this shape? _____

5 There is a sign saying that there is going to be a new monkey enclosure.
There are pictures of the different options:

_____ _____ _____ _____

Name each shape.

Which shape do you think would be best for the new monkey enclosure?
Think carefully about what monkeys like to do. _____

Explain your choice.

_____

_____

6 Two classes are visiting the zoo today.
Your class has 27 children in it.
The other class has 16 children in it.

Asif says, "There are 45 school children at the zoo today."

Is he right?   yes ☐   no ☐

Write a calculation to show why.

_____

7 Every day the female elephant, Jenker, has three feeds.
She is given 8 bananas in each of the first and second feeds.
She is given 5 bananas in the third feed.

The keeper tells the class, "Jenker eats 21 bananas in total each day."

Is this correct?   yes ☐   no ☐

Write a calculation to show why.

_____

8 At the end of the day you visit the gift shop.
You buy a zoo stationery set that has the following items in:

What 2-D shape is the face of the ruler? _____

How many faces, edges and vertices does the eraser have?

☐ faces   ☐ edges   ☐ vertices

Sam says, "The pencil is a pyramid." Explain why he is **not** correct.

_____

_____

Visiting a museum

Your class is visiting a museum.
It has lots of interesting facts about different periods of history and a dinosaur display.

1 Your class meets at school and gets on a coach.
The journey takes 1 hour and 15 minutes.
You arrive at the museum at 10 o'clock.

At what time did the coach leave school?
Draw hands on the clock to show your answer.

2 The coach holds 58 passengers.
There are 27 children in your class.
8 adults have come to help on the trip.

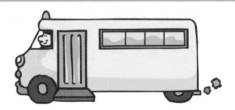

How many seats are empty on the coach? _____ seats

3 A child's ticket for the museum costs £2.

Child £2

How much does the school pay in total
for all the children to enter the museum?

£ _____

Box 5 on the next page features questions on measures. Talk to your child about the mass of objects in everyday situations. For example, when you are shopping give them two items and ask them to say which is heaviest / lightest. Look at labels on packets in the kitchen and discuss the use of grams (g) and kilograms (kg) for mass. This will help your child to understand the vocabulary associated with mass and start making comparisons.

4 You are given a map of the museum.
It shows that there are three floors.
There are 8 rooms on the ground floor.
There are 6 rooms on the first floor.
There are 9 rooms on the second floor.

How many rooms are there at the museum? ☐ rooms

5 There are three models in the dinosaur room:

Tyrannosaurus Rex   Stegosaurus   Diplodocus

255 cm long $2\frac{1}{2}$ m long   380 cm long

Which model dinosaur is the longest? _____

Which model dinosaur is the shortest? _____

Put the lengths in order to complete this number sentence:

☐ > ☐ > ☐

There are three fossils in a display case:

Fossil A   Fossil B   Fossil C

8 kg   695 g $7\frac{1}{2}$ kg

Put the weights in order to complete this number sentence:

☐ > ☐ > ☐

6 You enter the human body room.
The sign says that children of your age take 20 breaths per minute.

How many breaths would you take in 5 minutes? [ ] breaths

Another sign says that adults take 15 breaths per minute.

How many breaths would an adult take in 5 minutes? [ ] breaths

7 There are 26 bones in one human foot.

How many bones does a human have in both feet in total? [ ] bones

8 There is a machine that records the time it takes to run a set distance.
You run the distance in 12 seconds.
James runs the distance in 15 seconds.
Arif runs the distance in 11 seconds.
Mr Slade, your teacher, runs the distance in 10 seconds.
There is a sign saying,
"A cheetah would run this distance in 5 seconds.
A snail would 'run' this distance in 245 seconds."

Put all the names and times in the table to show the order from fastest to slowest. One has been done for you.

Who / what	Time in seconds	
		Fastest
		↓
Snail	**245**	Slowest

9 You go to the museum shop.
There are lots of items for sale:

30p   30p   50p

80p   25p

Freya bought a notepad and a pencil.

How much did she spend? [ ] pound [ ] pence

Freya had £2 to start with.

How much change did she take home? [ ] p

Max bought 2 postcards and 1 ruler.

Did he spend more or less than Freya? more [ ] less [ ]

Show your working.

_____

_____

Ahmed bought a pencil sharpener and a ruler.

How much did he spend? [ ] p

Ahmed had 1 pound and 50 pence to start with.

How much change did he take home? [ ] p

Choosing a pet

You have finally been allowed to get a small pet.
You must choose a pet and buy everything you need to look after it.

1 You have saved £30
Your mum and dad have given you £50
Your grandparents have given you £25

How much money do you have to spend in total? £ ____

2 You go with your mum and dad to the pet shop.
These are the animals you see:

rat £20   **rabbit £40**   **hamster £15**   **tortoise £100**

guinea pig £75   **gecko £60**

Which animal costs the most? _____

Which animal is the cheapest? _____

Thinking about cost, why would it be a bad idea to buy a tortoise?

_____

How many rats could you buy for the same price as one gecko?

____ rats

When adding two-digit numbers, encourage your child to add on from the larger number, e.g.
50 + 25 rather than 25 + 50.

3 At home, you have a table where your pet's home will be placed.
The table is 120 cm × 60 cm.
These are the lengths and widths of the homes you see:

rat	rabbit	hamster
70 cm × 50 cm	120 cm × 65 cm	60 cm × 55 cm
tortoise	**guinea pig**	**gecko**
80 cm × 70 cm	140 cm × 80 cm	50 cm × 50 cm

The tortoise home will not fit on your table.

Explain why.

_____

_____

Which animals' homes would fit on the table?

_____

_____

4 You cannot decide between a hamster and a rat.
The cost of the hamster home is £60.
The cost of the rat home is £50.

How much would a rat and its home cost? £ ⬚

How much would a hamster and its home cost? £ ⬚

Which combination of pet and home is cheaper?

rat ⬚   hamster ⬚

5 You decide to buy a hamster and a hamster home.
You have £30 to spend on everything else.

water bottle £3

food bowl £2

food £6

sharpening stone £3.50

sawdust £2.50

exercise wheel £5

toy roller £3

stairs £2

bath £3

hammock £8

overhead house £6

You must buy a water bottle, food bowl and food.

How much do these items cost in total? £ ☐

You must also buy sawdust, a sharpening stone and an exercise wheel.

How much do these three items cost in total? £ ☐

How much of your £30 have you now spent? £ ☐

6 You can choose what you spend the remaining money on.
What do you choose?

_____

Why did you choose this / these items?

_____

_____

7 Each day your hamster eats about 20 g of food.

How much food does he eat in 5 days? [ ] g

A bag of food holds 300 g.

How many days will one bag of food last for? [ ] days

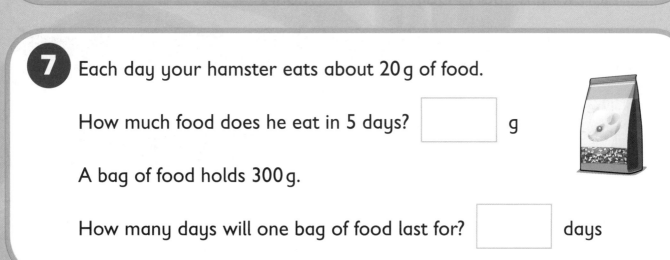

8 Your hamster spends $2\frac{1}{2}$ hours a day in his exercise wheel.

How many hours of exercise does he do in 2 days? [ ] hours

How many hours of exercise does he do in 4 days? [ ] hours

Sports Day fun

Today is Sports Day at school.
There are lots of races and everyone's parents have come to watch.

1 Sports Day is due to start at one o'clock.
It will finish at quarter past three.

How long is Sports Day? [ ] hours

2 There is a relay race.
In each team there are four children.
There are 10 teams running.

How many children are in the race altogether? [ ] children

In the obstacle race there are seven obstacles for each team.
There are five teams.

How many obstacles are there in total? [ ] obstacles

There are 50 parents.
They have to get into teams of five.

How many teams will there be? [ ] teams

Use objects to help your child understand multiplication and division. For example, lay out 7 counters to represent the obstacles in the obstacle race. Then lay out 4 more lines of 7 counters to show the array for 5 × 7. Use the array to show the link between multiplication and division, i.e. 35 ÷ 7 = 5 and 35 ÷ 5 = 7. If your child can picture the numbers, they will find it easier to answer questions such as these.

3 Each child will need two drinks during the afternoon.
In your team there are 12 children.

How many drinks will be needed for your team? [ ] drinks

4 Halfway through Sports Day the scores look like this:

Team	Points
Blue	67
Red	78
Yellow	86
Green	76

Which team is winning? _____

Which team is in third place? _____

How many more points does the Yellow team

have than the Blue team? [ ] points

5 At the start of the day, the headteacher took the
temperature on the field.
It was 16 °C.
In the break, he took the temperature again.
It was 23 °C.

Has it got hotter or colder?

hotter [ ]   colder [ ]

What is the difference between the two temperatures? [ ] °

6 In the break, the PTA sold ice-creams.

The table shows how many of each flavour were sold:

Flavour	Tally	Total
Vanilla	卌 卌 卌 卌 卌	
Chocolate	卌 卌 卌 卌 卌 卌 卌	35
Strawberry	卌 卌	

Write the missing totals to complete the table.

How many ice-creams were sold in total? ☐ ice-creams

Draw a pictogram on the lines below to show the information in the table. Use this picture to represent 5 ice-creams:

7 After the break, there is a sprint race.
The results are shown below:

Child	Time (seconds)
Kara	22
Jonah	20
Oscar	19
Raphael	21
Hannah	25

Who ran the fastest? _____

Who ran the slowest? _____

Write the names in order, starting with the slowest.

_____

8 At the end of Sports Day,
the number of points scored
was shown in a graph:

Use the graph to complete the
table and show the final scores.

Team	Points
Blue	
Red	
Yellow	
Green	

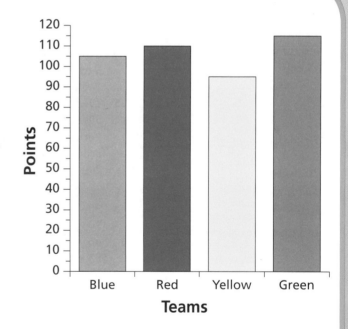

Tick the team that won.

How is this different from the half-time scores?

_____

Answers

Travelling by bus

1 20 people
2 7 people
3 8 people

Page 5

4 7 + 9 = 16 or 9 + 7 = 16
   19 − 7 = 12
5 28

Page 6

Going to a cafe

1 16 customers
   19 customers
2 11 customers
   16 customers

Page 7

3 16 cakes
   7 slices
   13 slices
   20 slices
4 15 doughnuts

Page 8

5 20 slices of toast
   4 slices of toast
   15 mushrooms
6 9 boxes

Page 9

7 12 balloons
   9 chairs
8 5 slices
9 30 sweets
   £12

Page 10

Going on a country walk

1 $\frac{1}{2}$

2 $\frac{1}{4}$

3 6 cm

Page 11

4 30 cm

5 $\frac{1}{3}$

6 $\frac{1}{4}$

7 yes
   $\frac{2}{4}$ is the same as $\frac{1}{2}$ and 6 is half
   of 12.

Page 12

Going on holiday

1

   late

Page 13

2

   5 minutes to 3 in the afternoon /
   5 to 3 pm
3 100 cars
   20 empty spaces
   80 cars

Page 14

4 5 minutes to 7 in the evening /
   5 to 7 pm
   swimming
5 £9
   50p
   Various answers but the coins
   drawn must add up to £1, e.g. 50p,
   20p, 20p and 10p

Page 15

6 90p
   90p
   no
   £3 + £2 = £5, which is more than £4
   yes
   2 pounds and 80 pence is less than £4

Page 16

Visiting the zoo

1 tiger
   koala bear
   quarter turn clockwise, walk
   in straight line, quarter turn
   clockwise, walk in straight line

Page 17

2 lions, monkeys
   4
   trapezium / quadrilateral
   yes

Any reasonable explanation about
the shape being an oval, which has
2 lines of symmetry.
Any one of these lines drawn:

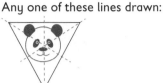

3 light
   cuboid
   cylinder − 2 (curved) edges

Page 18

4 squares, triangles
   squares, rectangles
   hexagonal prism
5 cylinder, cylinder, cuboid, cube
   tall cylinder
   Monkeys can climb. (Accept any
   other answer with a sensible
   explanation)

Page 19

6 no
   27 + 16 = 43 (not 45)
7 yes
   8 × 2 = 16, 16 + 5 = 21 /
   8 + 8 + 5 = 21
8 rectangle
   6 faces, 12 edges, 8 vertices
   A pyramid has a square / polygon
   base and triangular faces that
   meet at a point.

Page 20

Visiting a museum

1 (clock)

2 23 seats
3 £54

Page 21

4 23 rooms
5 Diplodocus
   Stegosaurus
   380 cm > 255 cm > 2$\frac{1}{2}$ m

   8 kg > 7$\frac{1}{2}$ kg > 695 g

Page 22

6 100 breaths
   75 breaths
7 52 bones